I0170312

Under the Water Was Stone

Poetry by
William Stratton

Winter Goose
Publishing

Winter Goose Publishing
2701 Del Paso Road, 130-92
Sacramento, CA 95835

www.wintergoosepublishing.com
Contact Information: info@wintergoosepublishing.com

Under the Water Was Stone

COPYRIGHT © 2014 by William Stratton

First Edition, May 2014

Cover Art by Winter Goose Publishing
Photograph Courtesy of William Stratton
Typeset by Odyssey Books

Paperback ISBN: 978-1-941058-14-5

Published in the United States of America

For my father

Contents

Family

Float

If I had drowned in the rolling black waters of the Chenango,
passing down the valley between the county roads, my hands
palm down, my face drawing the muddy bottom upwards
with litters of old leaves and rotten logs, the bloated white
of my skin dark against the snowed banks, all of time left to me,
but no longer me to enjoy or suffer it; if it had been me dragged
inexorably towards the Atlantic, destined to feed the bottom
feeders or be dredged from a canal, no story I tell now,
nor all that I might come to tell would be enough
to soothe you, to keep the scuffed pine floors silent,
to remove the thought of my ghost from your house
and every November the cabin would seem barebacked
and rotted, the thick limbs of the hanging hemlock
or the stained four-by-fours would sit mutely on one another
begging for the fire, and I know there would be no easing
early February, and my brothers could do nothing for you
but sit and watch the gray weight yoked to your shoulders,
and bring on occasion a glass of single malt to brown your lips.

I have spent so much time in error, formulating a space for you
to inhabit, making a bed that is not yours, preparing a home
for you to visit, planning grandchildren you will not hold,
but this is not what you have left me, no more than if
the slow waters allowed me residence, I would leave it for you.
I am sorry for my grief, and I promise to let it pass from me,
if I have the strength to rest it at the memory of your feet.

Blood

First I saw his trailer, jackknifed across both lanes.
In the fog it looked like the horses had broken free
on a dead run; there was hay for a quarter mile
spread out atop the skid marks,

as if the state boys had wanted to seed the black pavement
for spring. It was beautiful—the wet air, the easy valley sides.
I held his grayed head to my suit jacket. We did not speak,
my slacks blossoming dark under his opened body.

Rises

This curved stream
holds pockets whose lint
are trout. Hiding
behind waving blades of grass,
I see the shape of my father—
squinting against the low sun
and casting flies that flit and bobble
on rills forming over rocks
or logs. We share a passing strike,
then another, and if no mouth rises
we are content
to watch the water
slide towards the sea
and let the light sink
slowly into evening.

My Father's Garden

You imagined tomato plants through the snow,
planned your garden in February, moved the roto-tiller
out into the frostbitten yard. I was looking
for evidence of spring in the frost lines,
shaking the frozen hose and wishing for more light.

Barrel-chested and hungry you
marked off rows and laughed
at my crooked lines. Now I watch
the nights shrink and think maybe

if I had learned a little more I could grow your body
by August, have you back for a summer storm.
On the porch your empty rocking chair moves.
This year I will take it into the yard and plant it by May.

Grandpa

"Nothing is a something, it'll suck you dry
as the whisper you can hardly hear that tells you why."
—*Chris Smither*

Forty years ago I lost my arm
up on the hill to the corn picker,
walked the mile back to the house
with my belt around my arm.
I tied it with my teeth and dialed
the operator with my good hand,
but I never felt like I lost anything
till I put down the bottle
and picked up the farm again,
colder, less a few pounds, sober.

It was a long mile—I thought about the hay
catching fire and tearing through the loft,
raining down on my heifers,
and I felt my missing hand grip
that husk for the last time.

Last year my son drove his truck
into a pond. His last words a thank you
for the drink his friend poured.
I never died from feeling the lack
but I gave unwillingly my son
to the empty space the booze opens.

I know I have one more drink in me.
This past Thanksgiving, I asked my grandson
for one last bottle, scotch. I want to drink it
on my deathbed, and remember his father.

Albert

In the hour before the bus came it was just us
and the wilds of King Settlement Road.
Your stories I remember as legends:
the days when you lost your finger,
your wife, your sons, your farm
to lust and consumption and war and fire.
The heat of summers spent in the hay rows,
silvered guns you gave your grandson—
my father. The stone foundation holds; the floors
remind me of your frame, bent, hunched.

It must have pained you. Your neighbors dying,
your cows gone, your barns ruined, the fields
overgrown with alders . . . even the CCC trees
falling in your wake. Near the end you thought
I was your brother, tall and lean and angry.
I dream of you with my father, joined soon by your son.
The three of you walking the property line;
measuring stone walls in strides, stopping on a ridge
to listen for the call of a bobwhite, or the bleat of a doe,
or baying cows in pasture. Hold them
in the dawn of their departure.
Soon I will wander old logging roads,
ducking under apple boughs and black locust
thorns, though no ghost needs to fear
the dark space beneath a fallen oak,
or thick alder swamps, or the limestone cave behind
a ribbon waterfall, or night in the tamaracks.
I have waited so long to talk to you again
one more morning will not silence me.

Earl

Today I rose slowly, a pull I had not felt before in my body—
the bed, my back, my age. Not agony,
but not painless. At the table my wife had laid out
my morning cookies, my coffee, my newspaper,

just as she always did—a simple thing to be pleased
about. I listened to her putter around the kitchen
as I penned slowly in large letters the answers to
the crossword. Outside the day broke clear and mild.

In the shower I remembered autumn in Pennsylvania,
frost on the brown leaves, the hunters moving in flocks
towards open spaces, the way the hour before a snow
felt in the chest, heavy and fallen and damp.

There were always trucks on the street, the milk truck,
the fire truck, the trucks that moved the coal from here
to the train and back again empty, like the towns later,
sucked dry of life and death both, the life of the people
and the death in their black lungs—

the old waltzes drifted in and out of my mouth,
and I sang them softly in rhythm to the falling water,
as I was falling; the shower could not catch me,
and I could not catch myself. I was too old.

When I fell it was the hard rim of the sink, my head,
and the darkness of the Pennsylvania night
leading me again to the cold autumn morning.

Bus

Her hand brushes my leg—
she murmurs an apology.
I murmur back something gentle, an excuse . . .
we speak almost to ourselves.

Across the street the autumn light
reflects flatly off oak leaves,
someone pulls aside the attic curtains.

I hear her clicking away
on a pink smart phone,
her thin fingers delivering
in segments some message—
I remember my grandfather
in his old office, now fitted with a yellowed bed
and festooned with coffee mugs, a machine to measure out
in doses the liquids his kidneys need,
his feet swollen like gourds.

"Everyone knows they're going to die," he says.
"But not everyone believes it.
"Well, goddamnit,
"I believe."

Closing My Eyes To The Light
Of An Autumn Morning

Because I teach at eight in the morning
I am awake early enough to see on occasion
the sun rise. Sometimes I can catch it
over the water. Those mornings
I think about my father. He loved the early
hours, he used to tell me they were the best
part of the day. I think he held always
in some part of his heart the first light
from his childhood—the only time
to be alone on the farm, just him and
the cows. The world must have seemed to
belong only to itself, and he with it.

Yesterday morning I lost my grandfather.
It was a morning like this one,
clear and sharp and close to the equinox.
The light slants haphazardly this
far north, this close to autumn, this early
in the day. They can be together now, if
you believe in that sort of thing. I do, I think.
Maybe the soul has always been pure energy,
rising from the body so regularly we have
forgotten it is something which can fill us
with awe. It was early when he died. Though
he was not there, the horses woke and wanted
feeding, the cows wanted pasture. It was time
for chores. It was time to let go, the world
belonging only to itself, and he with it.

Plum

The morning after my father died
I had not slept. The yard was gray and green and wet
and lit in the way things are before the sun has risen.
It was June: the grass long, trees too full—
waiting for him to trim them. Everything
was waiting; the dog lay with her head on her paws, eyes open;
the house full of mourners still awake
in beds; the coffee brewed itself
as it did every morning;
I thought the silence might beg for an ending.
On the table, a single ripe plum.
I could do nothing but stare. I had never noticed before
the tiny galaxy on its underside; the imperfections
of its skin like white suns of other worlds,
the indent of stem a drain or black hole.
I held it a long while, until the house began to stir
and the legs of my family moved about the kitchen.
Then, I put it back on the maple counter, and turned away.
I felt it behind me—
I could not take even one bite.

Poem #1

I imagine you atop the gunwales,
tilted towards the deck with each risen wave,
caught between falling and flying.
Your belly full of me,
at home with the sea all around you,
the wind pulling hair across your face
like foam playing about waves.
Behind you my father, stern and wild,
free at last in the storm's breath.
Mostly you though, my beautiful mother,
all the violence of your youth
back with the hills and farms,
while the swell of your body
rises and falls with that of the water.

The Birds My Father Loved

He would sing them melodies
from his "way back when,"
and through the window could see
the tiny motions their heads made,
the dark colors of their eyes, the muffled
sounds of their feet on the grooved bark.

It is quiet at his house all winter now.
I sometimes wonder if a few birds died
that first year without him. Used to being
fed every day they may have starved;
the wildness they had lost returning, sudden.

Looking in as they ate their breakfast,
knowing the mountain of him was
gone forever, sitting on the empty
branches and seeing at last the drifts
and how high they are, feeling
through puffed feathers for the first time
the cold.

The Elm

There was not much to say.
The car hummed and in front of me
the world came into focus, light crept
from the gray sky and I had nothing to offer.
We looked for deer or turkeys or coyotes, foxes—
but mostly there were old farms
along the road, the people
cast out, the cows butchered or sold,
the barns sagging. Everything confused me;
I did not know about dying even if
I knew about death.

                       Still, there was
on the top of one hill a tree
my father called *his* tree; an elm
which survived the dutch disease
by living in the middle of a field
alone. It was a giant,
thick enough to hold against the wind
such a spot suffered, it shivered and
bent but never broke.
The world around it was empty,
especially in snow—the drifts climbed
its trunk and leaned. I wondered if
it would be there as I grew into a man,
if I could come back when I needed
something hopeful. I wanted it to live
another hundred years. Nothing
lasts. I noticed it was gone the same summer
my father took the car and put it
into the pond and both died there.
I suppose someone took its body
down and cast it into a fire, somewhere.
I imagine the flames singing, if only
whoever was there could have heard them.

Friends

Beloved

Face Down Days

I have seen the weather grieve, seen
it tear a woman apart,

the ropes that bind her body
to the world snapping taut ends.

I know well the faces met
at funerals, the stares of the bereaved

taking, always taking, and the way
the lines of mourners seem to snake

into the past, constricting the moment
where you live, and the other does not.

I have seen myself in the mirror
unshaven, addressing no one

in the deadened days
which those who have survived

must face down one by one.
I am writing to say: I hope you die first.

If one of us must sit,
on a faded porch of the future,

trying to remember the curve of a jaw, or the feel
of something soft on the lips, I want it to be me.

Torn

Tonight, staring into the bathroom mirror,
I feel my hand brush something small
into the sink—a Coquina shell, its worn edge
pale and broken, thin. It makes a slight noise,
not wanting to protest the water.

I am terrified to lose you.
What will my sink be
when you die? Plain, hard,
stained where I reached too quickly
for a fallen shell, and my finger
tore on the jagged faucet.

Things She Should Have Said During The Wake

He was a good man. He was
full of laughter. Once, I saw him
in my Carharts, smiling chagrined and guilty.
He was louder than my anger.
Though I barely knew him after all, I knew
none of it was real for him:
the steel in his worked hands,
the dark bottles empty on the wall, the needle;
all through a mirror or lens, belonging to someone else.

If it had been me who found him
on the porch, if I had seen him that last morning
I might not have pounded his chest
or kissed the air into his lungs
but rather let him be still
as he never was when I knew him alive.

Suck

It ain't the way it looks, Brandon always said about the blood, it's the iron taste. Even when it didn't get to your mouth, it was on your hands, in your shirt collar, when you're really sucked out. Every wrestler sits in a chair while he showers, standing takes too much out of your body, which is eating itself, so with skeletal hands we turn the nozzle all the way to the left and burn the hate off our skin. Most people sit in chairs all day but ours were thrones of misery, the water everywhere and we were so dry we would have killed our own mothers for one fat, lazy drop to hit our mouths. Go ahead, Brandon would say, drink a little. But even a mouthful would be a few ounces I didn't have to spare, so our noses bled in unison as the showers broke over our hunched and bitter ribs and all the while Brandon would talk about what it tastes like, the only thing we could drink without gaining any small part of a pound.

Feeding

All day I ran with pretty
blond boys who kept locked
away the things I wanted:
guitars, shoes, clothes, girls.

We danced on the brown grass
and tore through the dust
pulling up storms, we rode
the trails unafraid—lighting

the trees with fire streamers,
drank the still water in noiseless gulps,
watched the days fade until we came
to our bunks. They slept the sleep of

what? I did not know, I was
lying awake, shining a flashlight
out my window, attracting flies
and moths, watching them caught

in the spider's web, watching them turn
slowly into hollow, gray-kissed cocoons.

After The Crash That Ruined
Your Bicycle

For Patrick

On the lawn a father teaches his son to kick a ball.
The boy, knee-high, stumbles here and there,
his tiny foot missing the ball as much as making contact,
his brightly colored fleece flashing in the diffuse autumn,
leaves blowing around him, a fresh nip on the westerly wind.

Think of the people who might be
unable to enjoy a day like this—
the movements of the seasons,
in which a man and a man-to-be
learn about the wideness of the world
in the roundness of a thing,
are reminders of something fragile,
slippery, and for some,
faded in the infancy of afternoon.

One, turning his head
on a hospital pillow
might think
this is not it,
this is not
what I meant,
at all.

Prepostion: Of

For Duncan

Used to indicate possession, origin, association
We belong together, you and I. The same substances make me
that make you. We connect, us both,
not only to each other, but things to one another:
Words suffice for you, I use my body.

About, concerning
Speak to me about love.
About your mother's womb.
About planes, clowns,
washing machine dreams,
telephone poles, Narnia.
Speak to me concerning nothing,
it makes no difference,
so long as I can hear your voice, I am with you.

To indicate separation, as in time or space
Finally then, you can leave me, on the table at the bar,
drowning in the circles your drink made.
I will wait for you here alongside *about, to, at, without.*

Portrait Of The Alcoholic As
A Young Artist

His hair, tangled blond curls that rode his brow wild,
smelled of air and sweat and booze all at once.
Probably his dirty jeans and black suit jacket
were fashion statements I did not understand,
a torn-and-tumbled look. He was drunk. It was six in the evening.
He strode across Main Street oblivious
and saluting smartly toward the receding car horns,
his hands steady, his gait assured. On the bus he talked about
never feeling so good, about bitterness, about the wreck
he was constructing of his tomorrow. He asked me about
drinking with him, but I have a fear of alcoholics,
or at least of drinking with them. It seemed later than it was.
Outside, the streets were sporadically lit and unlit,
the early evening traffic coasted by, people doing
the Tuesday shop, the Tuesday yoga class. The Tuesday
get drunk and vomit on the side of the bus,
most likely not on their to-do list.

I want to enjoy my obsession, he told me.
And I knew what he meant.

Homer In The Kitchen

There are no poems for Jared.
Not even this one,
which I doubt he will read.
There is no insurance sestina
no pink slip sonnet
no gas prices haiku
for mostly the same reasons.
Even if there were,
he is uncommonly uninterested
in the language of verse.
With five children
and a cook's wage
he has enough tangles
in his life
without twisting his calloused fingers
into the convoluted words
of higher writing,
which belong in large part
to the kind of people
that eat at his restaurant
but never once take the time
to put in a good word
for the hands that made
their pâté.
I can hear Jared
in the kitchen, yelling
at the waitresses *for*
fucks sake bring me
something immortal
to read while I
burn this steak
but even Homer,
with his Gods and men

of greatness, would be as
helpless as I
to plate such a dish
as the everyday.

Self

My Last Words

I have already uttered them, unknowingly,
though they sit apart now in some disorder
awaiting the proper moment to unite.

Perhaps already I have poems that contain them,
a narrative embedded in something self important
which on that day I will be ashamed to admit
is grandiose and wholly insufficient.
Perhaps I have spoken them on the phone to my mother
as words barely words, but in a language
only that bond could pass in understanding;
or engraved them into some table when I was younger,
in passion to some cause I can not remember.
Perhaps I will simply slip on an untied lace
and the long-awaited words will consist
of no more than a few vulgarities
as I float down the stairwell.
On that distant day perhaps
I will be inspired beyond what I am now capable of.
It is no good to speculate.

I hope I will think of some other day
when those words and I had
a better time of it, when I sat on the bank
of some slippery river and watched the water
dive down the arced stones towards sunset,
never once stopping to whisper any farewell.

White Lines

We wanted the snow to fall in
the night, but it waited and came
instead all morning in furious
bursts; one moment we were
red and orange and camouflage
and the next we were white.
I shook flakes the size of dimes
from my shoulders and dusted
clean my hat over and over. I
wanted to pull up my gun and
fire into the woods at the blank
trunks of storm-blown trees or
run through the thick of them
and tear my face with blackberry
brambles, lose myself in the dark
Tamaracks and burrow into the
blow-downs, to crawl
out of the body of the hunter . . .
I wanted to be done with *me*,
to put away *I* and think instead
all, or *we* not because I loathed
myself or because I was tired
of killing, but because I saw
between the white lines of
falling snow something I had
not realized before was there
and it made me want to know
all I could about it. Then I
moved quickly away, back
to the flat-walled house. I sat
for a moment in the quiet kitchen,
staring out the terrible alien windows,
and wondered if I had stayed too long.

We Have Traveled This Way Before
And There Is Much To Be Learned

Today I woke and did the things I always do;
put on pants, checked the weather.
I broke an egg into a cold frying pan, poorly.
I could see fragments of shell through the clear white
on the black background. They dodged my finger
as I tried to help them towards the rim.
Then it was as if the egg had felt like something other—
the bend in a stream I used to walk along,
where it came from the brushy swamp
and cut away the side of the hill a few feet,
just high enough for me, if I lay on my stomach
to reach down and feel between my fingers
the water swift and cold,
or on the best days the soft white belly
of a trout, slipping as I tried to push it
towards the sun, the surface—
I had broken it.

Burnt

I drank scotch until the sun bled in slow waves from the east
and smoked camels from soft packs I could sneak
into my jacket, played the school courtyard for free,
ate Ramen noodles, and said fuck it, who cares,
and reveled in the answer: no one.

No one cared I was burning down my life with gasoline fingers,
I could drop a ten strip and run broken into the woods
or scrounge up enough empty cans to trade for a few full ones,
no one cared that at a party once I bit a man for calling me a fag
then smashed his head through the drywall
and tore up the house with a bowling ball I later tossed
through the window of a post office.

If I crawled up the highway signs
and pissed fifty feet down on passing cars
or passed out with a lit smoke in my mouth
and woke with a charred mattress
no one cared, and the freedom of it
was power I had not known was in me,
I was the brilliant filament left behind
from a blown bulb in a dark room.

Waving

Do you still write about death
I am asked,
as if I found the answer
and no longer needed to ask the poem.

If pressed, though, I would have said:
it's about a woman I saw once
and the lines on her face, her tears
and the way she stared at the waving limb
of a nearby tree;
the way it waved
and seemed to be saying goodbye.

I would have told them about how
even on a Saturday afternoon
in late spring
when summer is barely contained
and something unbearably green pushes
at the soles of passersby
there is a funeral, and we are mourners.

In Dreams My Hair Is Forever

My friends say I look like an Indian when I let my hair down.
It is black, my hair, it does hang straight down to my shoulders.
At times I have braided it and thought it was maybe even more
Indian than before. They tell me my great grandmother was
native, a Mohawk who came from another Mohawk and a half
breed French Canadian. She was given to a family who lived on
the Chenango. I imagine her in a white dress after that, from
the dirty clothes eight siblings passed down, I think she must
have thought this was what happened when you dreamed too
much, the dreams came to life and took you away from your
family. I know she was a dreamer, I mean, I know she had them,
the kind you have at night when your father has been drinking
again, stumbling through the dark kitchen reaching brown hands
towards brown bottles kept high on the shelves, instead of food,
instead of money, instead of soap; the sour treasure of whiskey
kept with the life of abandonment, extinction, love, stories and
then adoption, dreams which come and leave in their place a kind
of bursting, torrential lack, and which wake you, your eyes scan-
ning for movement on the dark shaped ceiling, thirsty and tired.
I try to think of her when I let my hair down, when my friends
say I look like an Indian, I think maybe she would like the way it
looks, it might remind her of being young again, being alive even,
it might remind her I came not just from the hard hands of the
farmers but also from the dark hair of the keepers of the flint.

Mellowfest

Every August I would lie on my back
while the music played, the blue stars
like drifting sunfish on a windless day,
behind them, oceanic, dark,
the waveless sky, the coral aurora borealis.
In my mind my life's adventures:
football on fields still wet from morning,
evening fires on the lake's edge,
hiding in shade from the afternoon sun . . .
I did not know then that not all adventures
end in gold. Around me the mountains went on
forever. I imagined I knew what the world was:
a great ship like those I saw anchored around
Albany Island, only one that moved,
to take me from some safe place
into the unknown. I think it was
a true story, though I cannot remember now
how it goes.

A Poem About Titles

or

Lines Written Above My Nameless Odes

or

My Life Sans Incipit Meaning

or

How I Orphaned My Words

or

Wrestling With The Angel Until Dawn, But Still Not Finding Its Name

or

What Kind Of Monster Refuses To Give His Writing A Label

or

Baptize, Dub, Christen, Denominate, Designate, Call: How I Failed My Readership

or

Rushing The Name: My Life As An Untitled Nobody

or

Yes, I Know I Take A Long Time To Title My Poems, But They All Get A Name Eventually

I would like to blame my parents.
As a child I was given a name so common even I
forgot it, and ever since, I have struggled to find
the perfect moniker for my work.

When wayward stanzas or lines beckon,
I listen; and inscribe above them the spoken name.
I do not ask the poem to rush.
It is already giving me
everything.

In The Room With Donald Hall

I thought you should know:
before you tottered in
the room was quiet; we sat staring reverently
at the empty podium. Outside it was
a faded autumn day
and yet the room was full,
as full as a small room
in the basement
of a public university library
can be.
You were so old,
I thought you might not make it
across the room,
even so, I knew that this was
as good as it gets.
That if I were really good
and lucky, and somehow
did not die of accident or disease
or lose my voice or mind or fade
into obscurity . . .
I too might someday gather
up to fifty strangers
to hear me talk about poetry.

And I have not even told you:
all the while as you spoke
I was devastated, wordless.

Bent Low

Long hours in the woods by myself,
hours with muddy trails crisscrossed by roots,
leading me to places I somehow know already,

the leaves falling lazily towards faded others,
the sounds of my feet making the calls of birds
into names I know, and do not know.

At different times of day and season,
I have seen the sun through branches,

over rises and drifts of snow, up wholly
from every pond, or shattered
by every stream, turned brown by river water.

Some things have no name,
things like a dozen strands of spider silk
above the waving timothy,

or the shade of a doe's eyes,
scanning the trail ahead, or my reflection in them.
I will not leave.

I know the weight—
the weight of one ancient oak,
fallen on a sapling of its own acorn.

Robin

I have cursed the robin, early riser
among early birds, have lain on my back
and denounced his orange vest,
his incessant repetition of song
while the dawn forms; a timid glow from
the center of the earth—there is nothing
timid in his iterations, the robin cries
more, and more, and louder.

Still I must admit—because
he is so common, because everywhere I have lived
has had at least one robin-in-residence,
in the wee hours with my eyes closed, I can be anywhere:
my worn college mattress adorning a trampled floor,
the sleeping bag that burned in the Adirondacks,
the house on Hunt Hill. In some moments
when I am near to sleep I step outside my heavy body
and forget that day is almost here . . .
I can be any*time* again, even years ago
when the robin first woke me
and I went into the dark yard of my father's house
to search the wet spring lawn for worms we took downstream
for a try at a few brookies in the first light before school,
while I wondered what kind of man I would be.

These Poems Are To Myself

At night birds whirl in the sky.
The stars behind them
blinking in and out,
the wind turning leaves up, down,
the smell of sleep
blowing from the trees towards the road.

At times light rises
on the horizon, but it is not day:
it is a car, or the moon,
or a trick of the eyes—
the blue and black linger, settle.
There is no one in the distance
calling to come out,
there is no voice of another.

Mare

Curtains know sound the same way
mothers know when their sons die far away
in war, sudden stir without wind, moment
of wakefulness in a dream, fading ripple
of the soul. In the room a man in a hat
holds a giant spoon with which he carves
the inside of a round melon, as he turns
it we see the melon has a face contorted
not in pain but in loss. At the altar a tattoo
has come to life and because it is a snake
writhes on the grip of a triangular knife.
All around, the windows are stained. The man
is revealed as a doctor, the curtains shiver.
Behind our wide mouths are rows of teeth
breaking, crumbling and we are sinking
as the thought of flight is replaced by doubt,
and we are the melon which is the only thing
left to eat. Here is how we know what we know.

Plenty, Hay

Much has been said already
on the subject of haying;
the chaff stuck to wrists,
blistered lines on the palm, the line
between red and white skin
where the sleeves of a torn shirt end;
none of these are revelations.
Revelations . . . And what did I expect?
To me, the heat was unbearable, the days
seemed to never end and the fields too,
immense and pitched on the side of hills;
my grandfather would lead a parade:
tractor, baler, wagon, and my long arms
reaching down with a hook
to snag the slowly birthed squares of dead grass—
I was tired of it even in the early hours
and by evening, having torn my arm
on a protruding piece of metal or
had the bald wagon tire bruise my thigh,
no feeling of great worth came over me
as the dark came over us.
I was less than sullen, but less than convinced too
of the value of such a thing—piling
five hundred or so bales
into the loft seemed to me just
a thing to do in order that my father
might hand me a few dollars
and leave me alone a short while.
Today though, I sat on the deck
and watched the spring wind toss
the pale leaves back and forth,
and smelled for the first time since August
cut grass and fumes and felt a little heat

on my face, and I was ashamed for myself,
to know that I had spent a few days
in the perfection of the world:
my body harvesting the wealth of the sun,
the dark earth, the water, the seed . . .
and I had not known what it was
when I was in it; something as pure
as I would ever know. Behind my house
the barn has tilted and fallen, the fields
mostly empty, my father gone, my grandfather
not far behind. I remember they kept a few
hives in the hedgerow, and the smell of honey
would rise above the clover and timothy,
the sounds of the bees coming back into tune
when the ring from the machinery faded,
the taste of it too, and the cold water we drank
right from the creek, so cold
you could only take so much.

The World

"Ain't No Direction But One I Want To Go In, And Can't Never Get There"

On Fridays Willie would ramble in and find his favorite stool
to trade me half a paycheck three dollars at a time
and the regulars would crowd around to humor an old story
passed along the bar through tiny puddles, in hopes to catch
a round on the factory, before things got ugly
and some college kid walked in to the nest of local hornets
who stung worse than they buzzed.

But I never minded, even when the cops came
to take down my name and where I lived
in case the twenty-somethings pressed charges
which they never did—something about old men
made them heal quicker or forget faster or both—
I just kept pouring out Budweisers and Jamesons
hoping to take in another story of boxing or boozing or both—
until Willie's boxcar hands crashed into fists and curled onto faces
        or ribs,
the hardness of it all reminded me of rusty chain-link fences
and broken green coke bottles on lots where fires have burned
but now weeds grow tall as a man, and hardier, and more alive.

Horus

Down the street a man lives with a dog he calls
Horus, the tall house they live in has wrought-
iron railings on the roof and three chimneys,
one of which has a brick missing on the face
which faces the street. Horus is a mastiff and
when the man walks him people are often
afraid, so they have taken to walking at night,
down the streets in the dark, Horus striding
from stoop to stoop and the man behind
glancing towards lit windows and at every
pair of headlights turning his face away.
One night they do not come around,
and for a week no one sees them. Some
whisper the man has died, or moved away.
The neighborhood cannot decide what to do,
each person in their beds at night wondering
what had happened to Horus and ashamed
they knew the name of the dog and not its
owner. Then finally someone sees the man
at the hardware store or at least they think
they see him but no Horus. The man is buying
nails and rope and then the next morning
they see a giant painting made on many
sheets hanging from the roof. It is of Horus,
his right eye the sun, his left the moon, his
droopy ears stretched to wings, his long dog
nose pinched to a hooked beak. It hangs
all day and week and month until one night
the man goes outside and humming
softly to himself puts a match to it. Then
he stands back and watches Horus ascend.

Behind The Bookstore

A bird lay in the short grass, mangled from
a fall or a brush with a car. Blood came
from its body, its wings bent irrevocably. Still,
it clung to life, a few boys poked at it
with sticks and hefted small rocks.
It tried to crawl some, towards the trees.
Their cruelty must have shown on my face—
I could see us mirrored in their eyes, some turned
partly away. None spoke.
How might I look, lying on the side of the road
bent badly and unable to drag myself to quiet shade
and die in silence? I could do nothing for the bird
or the boys but to end it. I felt
the hollow bones under my shoe. The boys
barely moved as I pulled away. One waved.

Seven Gun Salute

It was close to nine when we came out,
many had spoken eloquently, their words
spilled down the aisle and broke
into rivulets on each pew, over bent heads
and under bent knees. We came out
into the wet darkness of September—
in the rectory lawn was a small pillar
and a tightly wrapped American flag.
I moved onto the street, I could not face
the seven men with their guns, I could not
bear to see the faded uniforms pressed
neatly, the creases bent and the waves of people
breaking over them, generations having
broken over them and gone now. I stood
accidentally in front, they pointed
the blank barrels over my head towards
the southern stars. Each volley sounded
true against the neighborhood houses.
Each volley broke the words we had left
in the church and cast them out against
the world like pale shrouds. I held my ground
as best I could. I bent double, I bent towards
the river and looked up. I wept
behind the sound of taps, where no one could
hear me. What kind of life had this been?
I know the war left bottles in its place,
emptiness, torn places a man puts
inside himself. War leaves war behind
like a package, go ahead: unwrap it;
or go ahead: leave it. I went to shake their hands,
each one having fired three rounds out
and having seen only the muzzle flash.
I thanked them each. Most nodded.

I felt each was afraid to speak
at all; as if any word might transform
into a howl. They wanted to scream but couldn't.
One spoke on behalf of the rest: "We're honored."
I was honored. I was in honor of them,
of their late night salute, of the fearless
facing of their own services, of the brass
shells they left behind. Goodbye, they had said
with the sharp reports. Goodbye.

Gull

On the beach a gull, eyes rolling
white and gray, watches the slow
roll of the tide, spreading pale arms
in vain attempts at sudden liftoff,
fearing the local dog, the teenage boys,
the ceaseless waves. Under its belly
both legs are useless. One broken, one
torn and hanging badly, wrongly.

A thousand tiny jewels of sand surround him.
Above, the stone woman who marks lost sailors
casts her shadow. The names of the dead
are carved at her feet. There is nothing more for them to say.

A Good Measure

A friend who is also a young poet
younger than me by a good measure
we were standing outside the bar
and he told me about the missing dead the violence Syria
and *how can I write about it* he asked me
and I thought about the reading earlier
there were poems about love,
swans, the single sound the world makes
and they were beautiful really
but no poems in regards to Syria no poems
responding to explosions men and women running
towards Turkey children caught up in barbed wire
marionettes of war and how could there be really
how could we write about them when for most
of us the worst part is the bit about how cold
it is and how short the days seem and damn
wont it suck to not have a job being a famous
poet? *Shit* I said and I meant it I don't know
how to write about what I do know I don't
know how to write about my own home about
the brown hills rolling away and away about the
skeletons of farms and trailer parks about
empty parking lots about the winding dark river
the poverty the small minded cruelty
the small town minds beautiful under the grime
and bitterness left when the jobs are gone the good ones
went to Ohio and now we have a bank and a school
but I met there some who had the brightest parts
of themselves removed so they could carry on
and even these things are good even these lives
are worth living we have at least our days
without someone shooting at us we have
most of our nights without explosions and

we have loyalty to each other we have
mostly a life we can live without the missing dead
shit I don't know I said *shit*

Frost

A still night.
Smoke rises from cigarette
to Milky Way.
Frost settles in.
Crinkled maple leaves
make crisp sounds as they strike

stiffening blades of grass.
It is tempting to think
that I will someday be as stark
as the twisted gray limbs, free,
feeding the cold ground with my past.

War Memorial

My grandmother says *we are all drawn to water.* Between us
the twisting haunches of a river, a dark snake reaching
as the arm of a man. *You are always writing about separation.*
Along the sidewalk is a memorial for the dead soldiers and all
along its plaque are the names like scars or laugh lines, JOSEPH
P HARMAN PFC is the wrinkle of a forehead and WILLIAM
D HOOPER SGT the curve along a cheek, a dimple line,
what things cannot leave a face. Each of them carried a gun,
each watched a tiny explosion from the barrel and an ounce
of lead trace its long finger across air and land and body.
Take for a moment the still picture as it reaches an arm, a hip,
a mouth, and nestles snugly into the retreating skin.
I must have been one of them, to stare this way, to stop along
the nowhere sidewalk and see the curved lines of their faces,
to smell the granite beneath, the rasp of the lichens
and the dark earth. *You are stuck back there on that hospital
lawn.* What I see is the lawn, forever in front of me.

Ode To The Cursor

When it appears,
a single vertical moment,
the possibility of words,
of all things and thoughts,
a billion metaphors
or images from worlds forever.
In one blinking instant
the universe unfolds
and then, like all things infinite,
disappears.

During The Wedding

The chapel wood gleams—polished, oiled.
The sounds coming down from the rafters: ourselves,
bouncing from the vaulted ceiling back to the pulpit.
Simple lamps as lighting, small indented bulbs . . .
Little sun comes through the stained glass
dark with pictures: a woman
holding a baby away from old men; the man that baby
becomes and the curling rivers of his blood; a supernova above
pasture at night—and dark as well from the names of
several hundred who died during the great
World Wars I and II, in Vietnam, in Korea.
What kind of men were they, who now
share the back-lit glass with Jesus?

I miss the weddings they
did not have, the children they did not raise—
the evening sky pierced by tiny lights
we share, and of course the chapel,
though I will walk from its belly to the sounds
of the thundering organ, and they will
never leave the stained glass of its windows.

Ropes

Rode out to where the trees grew twisted
like ropes, under me road bent and sagged
and I could feel the palm of it crowning out of
the wet ground. That was the year a late snow
froze the ladybugs—they dropped like
red tears from the trunks of trees in vast
numbers. I felt as though every other house
was fallen down, every plot of land abandoned
and overgrown. The black ribs of barns
littered the roadside, I was afraid for myself
and my life ahead; I gripped and turned the wheel
in sudden jerks. Past Pharsalia was a shack
with a beer sign and inside a woman with one hand
poured moonshine into dark glasses and when
I asked her *do you know how long the farms have
been empty for* she shook her head and turned
a silver dollar over and over on the bar. It was late,
I had work on Monday. That night I dreamed
the sunset lasted forever, and everything grew
pointing west; the ladybugs twisting into knots
that littered the earth and bruised its sodden face.

Temptation

In court today;
with the battered blonde
recounting her testimony,
boyfriend sitting mutely ten feet away.
The trespassing ex-husband
indignantly slandering his
own ex-family;
the aging alcoholic, swaying
in the court pews as if
in rapture, dressed in the
sweaty suit borrowed
from his sober past;
the arrogant teenager
recusing the officer who pulled him over
for reckless and drunk driving
after one a.m.
without a license;
the temptation to tell myself
that I am not of this lot
is great, but nevertheless,
a lie.

May

We hung out until morning on your porch when
crawling out of the woods came an emaciated dog
all bones and slouch. It was so broken I wanted to
load up the shotgun. I thought I may want a bullet
were I the dog, I thought I would ask for one
were he me, but you took him inside

and fed him milk and he lived a few good weeks in your
kitchen. I saw him wag once. I want to die
knowing something as sweet as milk waits for me,
touched by slightly cupped hands, by someone
who is not afraid to *be afraid* of dying, and not afraid
to watch it happen, and while it does, to love.

The Railing

The jays scream because they are the only birds left.
There are no acorns, the apples turn on the limb
and refuse to ripen, the bladed maple pods
coat the pavement in dark droves;
speech slows and sticks in the mouths of children.

At night rain blankets all:
the cat between the saplings,
the deer grazing in the graveyard.

Lovers in the intermittent light
of the high school parking lot come to blows.
An old man falls at the end of his driveway,
mail in his hands, and passersby will not look or help;
children lean from the railing of the bridge to scream at trains
and no one stops them, or tells them not to fall.
Winter is already tearing down with bleak hands
the refuse of summer. Something dreamt has laid down
its head, something else has awoken.

We Are As Birds

My favorite beaches are rocks. I imagine myself
with a thousand hands, each feeling the grass
the waves grow and leave behind, then scoops up
so it can toss its wild hair in the roaring water.
Each pool its own sea, endlessly filling
and emptying, mapped in trenches and brilliant
islands breaking the sunlight into fingers.
Hidden in the jewels of its own secrecy, which lay
around and under and in it: a door, a liquid arch
through which the old gods of water can look back
on the faces of we who dwell on land. My favorite
beaches are carved from constant motion, from them
something is always given and something is always lost.
Beaches where people do not belong except as leaping,
momentary birds, our wings replaced by eyes,
our feathers turned to fingernails as we flit and dart
between where the water will come or has been,
and for a while we are only guests on the doorstep of the eternal,
where we will be the ones who move away. Behind
us, the ocean takes its final stroll towards the moon.

The Way A Cow Dies

First a man takes a bolt pistol and puts it
on the imaginary line between where
the two horns would be if they hadn't been
cut off, the air pushes the captive bolt into
the forehead and then a spring retracts it,
the cow is stunned and usually knocked out
cold or near cold and the front part of the brain
is mashed up but not the stem; this is so that
the bleeding process is not interfered with, that
being the part where a man with a sharp knife
opens its throat and lays it on the slaughter
house floor near a drain, the heart continues
to pump even though the cow can't think
anymore, if it ever did. Where does it die?
On the drain? In the stall, when the bolt enters and leaves?
Maybe I never noticed before how alive
they were, nosing up flakes of hay,
staring straight legged out to the horizon.
Maybe I never noticed before the man with the knife,
the knife having been honed and honed
as a man would his own razor, the way
he holds it and paints the red line wide.
The wide open road pouring out in front of him,
the river crawling slowly to the dark sea,
the water deep red against the falling sun.

Home

King Settlement Road

The streets I grew up on: a solitary
gray scar named King Settlement
then County Route 29, the hills
drawing out and away on either side

farms mostly dead, here and there a trailer,
unfurrowed fields. The infrequent cars sped past
and never stopped. I rode my bike a few miles
south and passed every time

an abandoned house. The windows
we never smashed, its threshold
uncrossed, not from fear of ghosts
or police or neighbors (there weren't any)

but because it might look inside
like our own homes, and we
would have known for sure how fragile
our lives were, how close to the dark

doorway we hovered every morning
before heading out into the world.

Ugly

It was picture day and the boys had
Tommy on the yellow grass kicking spitting
yelling w*hat an ugly picture shirt what an ugly*
pair of picture pants don't your momma dress you
no more what an ugly—but that was the last ugly
I could take my gut was full of ugly noises
the whimpering ones the heaving ones the open
mouthed groaning ones beside the bed at night
because there wasn't a mom there for me
either and that was the last ugly I could eat so
I made some ugly on them and then it was their
ugly on my hands their ugly blood their ugly teeth
marks I still have and the last thing I said to them
as the one ran and the other just lay down and sobbed
was *he only got one shirt.*

A Murder

Out in front of the old school, on the terraces,
David was leaning against a railing by the steps,
behind him a ravine and run down houses.
The cool kid, older, he smoked and exhaled with purpose
towards me. But I was cool enough I suppose
to listen. *Yeah, I fucked her* he said
but I'm done with that shit,
crazy bitch, fourteen and already crazy—

But I liked him anyway, because he was cool
and deemed me worthy to brag to,
about her sweet little body . . . What did I know about sweet
bodies? Rotating through the school around me
as if I were a tiny dull sun.
April was beautiful, and I hadn't known what it meant
to be beautiful, never have
and David, he was beautiful and seventeen as seventeen can
only be, but I didn't know that either.
There on the terraces everything was beautiful.
The sky was full of early autumn,
the red oaks lining the school road just brown around the edges.
In them, crows sat waiting for the busses to pull out and away
when the feast of spilled chips and bread crusts
left behind by the students would be theirs.
What do you call them David asked
the pack of crows?

Cain

"I tried to tell them I didn't do it."
—*Delbert Ward*

When I laid my hands on him
I felt the whisper of air between us fade
into every morning from here on,
alone with a fog that broke into me
and came out my mouth and eyes
and turned them white as my hair—
whiter, as if I had become a giant dandelion,
the seeds of my body cast into the wind.
I began to die alongside him, and the land knew,
and our father . . . and the world was hushed,
small, searing. There are secrets I cannot explain
because I can barely contain the knowledge of them;
the first breath blown into the calf,
the way a hog will stumble around after
the bullet has reached its brain,
the way water leaks out of your cupped hands
even if they are pushed tight against each other . . .
I have only just begun to explore such things as these.

I learned about how every second holds
the powers of creation and death in equal measure,
and how the two are kin.
I cannot remember if I have killed my brother
or if he has died some other way: sleeping,
dreaming of a hand to press against his lips as he lay.

Shorty

I told them I'd never sell, when the houses moved in on me
from all sides, crowdin my chickens, pushin my cats
round the yard like pucks over the river ice. When I was a kid
we used to play just down over there, the Chenango flooded
the flats and left us perfect oval rinks with broken corn stalks
as goals, and then the farmers started to die and left bitter
children livin away in the city and sellin off the tracks of land
whose names I can't remember. Now I got my newspaper
and my little house made of pallets and logs, I built it myself.
The coal's gone with the trains, and I ain't got enough trees
to burn at winter so I been takin the tires from the dealership
next door, the old ones they don't use no more and burnin them.
Last winter I froze solid and that one city man,
what's his name, came before and told me I was going to die
out here and I might better just take the offer and maybe he was
right to say it, cause now I can see that there ain't many mourners
here to put me under the stones I grew up pushing around,
just that Stratton boy and his son whose name I cannot recollect.
Good boys, both of them. They look surprised sorta, standin over me
and my little red coffin, sayin things: 'Shorty this' and 'Shorty that'
but I don't know why, I done told them I'd never sell.

Edward Rulloff

"Hurry it up, I want to be in Hell in time for dinner."
—Edward Rulloff

Who walked the streets of Ithaca at night and stared open-mouthed
at the dark lake, wondering if it would recount to future generations
the philology an angel brought to him, by which the world
could forgive and forget his sins.

Who as a child taught himself to speak in tongues—Greek, Latin,
German, French, Italian, Hebrew, Sanskrit, and with no education
became a teacher, with no degree became a doctor.

Who did give to a wooden box wrapped in chains
his only wife and child, and with the boat danced gently
as they slid to the bottom of Cayuga—he sang
a song to them and swayed, then
a small tune, a chime, hungered from inside to out
and only those two could have fed it, and did.

Who ran from himself, the him who robbed a man and shot one,
the brilliance of a mind pinned open with nothing left to say
but to say that it was not him at all, but a hole, or a pin,
or a poor boy forgotten and so was eventually caught
and told to hang until dead.

Who on the day said: now is a good time,
and the hurrying then was what he had last wishes for,
though his neck would not break, and so for long minutes
he hanged and breathed raggedly, Edward Rulloff,
five minutes, ten, fifteen, and then finally dead.

Fire, Chenango County
Poorhouse, May 1890

The Pauper

The fire came from the bed of a sick woman
who died with a pipe in her hands.
I was screaming and crying and there was
a gentle breath on me like a dream,
but then the ceiling came down and I
had nothing to do but to watch
the walls burn to the ground.

The Porter

I woke with smoke in my mouth heavy like a curse.
The poor man who woke me already singed, eyes wilder
than a horse with a garden hose around its foot and twice as loud—
a great sucking sound from the hallway like a man
short on breath and the door bent bad and hellish and there wasn't
a way to save all them women or idiots. I had nothing to do
but to run, still in my bedclothes. The flames drove me back.
I could hear them roasting inside and it was too much,
so I left them and found a few of the lunatics,
some I had to wrestle out the door and others just came,
sat in the great lawn by the elm and chestnut trees, their faces
aglow and some smiling and some crying and some
just slack as if bored. I know that somewhere in the fire was some
son or another, some daughter who didn't even know it was a fire
after all, that they stood all up against the doors,
thinking if they could keep them closed, if they could just
shut the windows tight enough, never mind the melting glass,
the black soot like a blizzard, the floorboards shooting nails
into the air, if they could just keep it all out, they would all
be okay. There was a fire, and there was no fire.

The Farmers

We came around sometime in the night to the screams.
I went out to the front with my gun and saw the aslyum afire
and burnin' bright enough to light up all the way to town.
We had a few boys to help:
Ezra, Franklin, German, Irvin, Walter
and we went over with buckets and rope.
Didn't take long for the flames to eat the whole thing up,
but by then, we had *them people* tied up in the yard,
to the trees, to each other, to the ground. One or two run up
through the orchard and into the hollow, but we never chased them.

The Inmate

I knew where the congressman lived
from before I was locked up in a place I knowed
was doomed to ash and burnin' flesh.
I grabbed a hatchet on the way through the orchard
from some farm whose man had gone to the fire.

I done knocked on the door
and I yelled at him
to come out and fight me,
that he had run things around Preston
and Pharsalia long enough,
I had come from Hell to annihilate him.
Farm hands got me from behind
or I would have put steel in his skull.

The Commissioner

I saw the survivors being brought up to Utica to-day.
One of them had a burn on his hands that looked like
a giant spider, another less an ear. One looked up
into the sky the whole time, cowering, shaking, wet
in the crotch, and I saw the clouds there
wispy and dark, moving slowly around the summer sky.

Fight Outside The Howard Johnson's Circa 1994

They were at it.
We heard the nose break first,
heard it and knew that words like ball and toy
and run were no words for a thing like this.
We heard the orbital fracture,
saw the cheek lacerate, felt the eardrum burst—
scattered, wet, red.
We were becoming the violent aliens of the future;
quiet ended then,
we would never erase the sound
of bodies tearing bodies
behind the hotel, the dimly lit and faded
stone facade facing down to the blacktop.
Away in the town the streetlights hovered—
tiny wingless angels.
I wanted to do something, smoke a cigarette
or spit or say something tough. I could not
move. I could not look away.

Music spilled onto the yellowed street
lined with piebald cars rusted and old
and windows drooped like eyelids half open, half closed,
from which people glanced once
at the flurry of movement and
did not want to see, for sure, wanted to go home
and fuck or drink alone or pass out but most
just didn't care, most were numb,
just a few more boys killing each other
in the parking lot, nothing new to it.
I could have screamed,
I could have yelled fire,

could have thrown my body against the wall
until even the boys
had to stop and look,
could have made them
look, and stop.

Unnamed

Beneath me the water of an unnamed creek riffles by—
unnamed because there are so many here,
riffling because there is a dead boy
lying face down on the solid limestone bed.
I say boy because he must be eighteen
his body sprawled as if he had been chasing something
in the seconds it must have taken him
to fall the hundred or so feet.
He looks from behind and above
like a smaller child toddling after a wayward
moth, and I wonder if before he landed
he saw in the thin waters
that it was not a moth at all,
but the waving of his own fingers
and the moonlight, lilting slowly
from the gorge's edge and resting in spiral side pools,
and if this knowledge, that his own life—
cast from the bridge beautifully,
so beautifully they put up arcing blue fences
so that no one could attempt to be so beautiful ever again—
was a series of frenzied motions
in a chase for something serene, and illusional,
and if he remembered in the last moment
that beneath the water was stone.

I Can Write About It

From the quarry the streets
tilted precariously towards the river, dull, askew;
at night the yellowed lights on the street faded,
the fields dark, wild, and open for fires,
parties out where the roads ended,
pallets lit up with flames as high as
the hemlocks, pickup trucks with their doors open,
music playing—a fight or two,
running from the police in the woods
laughing the kind of laughter we thought we
lost at puberty, but had only
misplaced among the tired brick buildings,
the empty lots, the dead railroad, the dark ponds,
the dull moments spiked with dread;
like when Paul shot himself and his stepfather—
we heard it on the radio on the
way to school in the morning,
knowing there was an empty desk,
the picture of the gas station in the paper,
the background an antique shop gone out of business,
just another junk pile: broken furniture, record players,
walkers, televisions, bed frames, a cradle.
When we graduated and moved on,
some of us, what it was like to leave
some behind, in trailers, in apartments, in jail, in graves,
and knowing that none of us would ever really get out . . .
but it ain't the same as being there.

In The Yard

There are three movements they make,
my hands, on swinging the maul:
first to pull it to one side in preparation for two,
hefted above my head, and lastly the slide
from head to handle-end. I am rhythm,
precision, I am young again in the woods
with my father, watching the chainsaw
slide in slow arcs through the prostrate trunks,
I am alone in February making weight
for wrestling under the winter moon,
I am spotting rotted leafless tops,
peeling bark away in grafts.
                                                    The ash
splits clean in one swing, I open its
white belly—brook trout fished from streams
and fried in black iron pans with butter.
The maple is hard but brittle,
I feel with the head of the ax
when it will give; inside it has a narrow
straight grain. A shame to burn,
but my brother found it blown down
and broken. The oak I save for last. It is old,
half a dozen knots riddle each section.
It will ruin my palms with blisters.
These are not to be taken in half, I count
a dozen swings for each small slice
I separate, two dozen, thirty. They do not
let go, I leave small red prints when I pull
them apart. This is the life I was born to;
the smell of autumn and smoke, the whisper
across the yard of the coming cold,
the lingering pulse where the ax has been
and the hollow sound of it on the bones

of the trees. Later, I feel the pain
when the blister connects with the keyboard.
The world of my youth misses me, and lingers.

The Castle

We are still in the land of the bullthistle,
the land of the loam, the gravel, the land of hills pockmarked
with scrub and fields and blue slate and below them
the river, always whispering to *Hahgwehdiyu* who scooped from the body
of his mother the world and banished his brother
so that those who have lived could make from *Chenengo* our home.

Once, our fort stood here,
called *The Castle* by the whites—
now there is only a blue sign,
tilted and unread on the side
of *East River Road.* Nothing else
remains, not even
a skull, though from time to time
a local boy could find
while out meandering the river flats
in search of some secret place
the head from an arrow,
buried half in the ground, heaved by frost,
burned along one edge, used and broken
but still, when drawn along the finger,
able to give to the ground
one last drop of blood.

Some of us remain. Most have gone
and we are grateful to have been spared
the worst of it, the houses that breed like rabbits,
the gray scar of roads, the fires
that never extinguish. I have seen these men
come forward as if on a storm,
lightning in their arms and teeth like clouds—
I tell you that the heart of them is paler

than their skin, there is no color in a man who can
turn on a brother. They are their
own curse. They do not need ghosts to haunt them.

Untitled

I learned to swim the way all wrestlers do,
by drowning. Dropped overboard, the sunfish drifting lazily,
I looked up towards the dagger board
until I was fished by my ankle from Champlain,
my father's huge hand the hook I could not swallow.

I left Ithaca the last morning of August
before the sun could fully melt
the wet off the hills, before the bent leaves
dried. Every mile the greenest thing
I had ever seen through a window.
The rivers spilled like broken glass away from me.
For seven hours I lived seven years over:
the tight lines of ridges as they tumble down the valley,
the sugar maples on fire, a thousand
choral voices in a summer field,
the towering walls of plowed snow reaching the power lines,
trying to pull out one memory that could be forever.

I imagined the car beside me swerving at seventy
into my dashboard, and thought about how long
it would take my ghost to return
to haunt the commons, the waterfalls, the lake shore.
I made the ocean in time to see the tide,
bottlenecked and roaring out.

Now I am standing lock-kneed on the side of a highway bridge
one hundred feet above the Piscataqua River, feeding
the Atlantic, whose cold waves I imagine are closing
doors I cannot see, folding them onto the darkened beach
where I will not find them.

Acknowledgments

This book is many years in the making, and so many people contributed to my growth as a poet and writer that nothing I can say will adequately address the gratitude I feel. Still, I must try, with apologies to those not mentioned in specificity here due to space restrictions.

My mother, who gave me my voice. My brothers and sisters. Nana, my aunts, uncles, cousins, grandparents, and the rest of my large and amazing family, including those who have passed. My friends from home (they know where home is) who are as loyal as any man could ask for. Dudley, the world and people it gave to me. The writers of UNH, poets and otherwise, who I miss terribly. My mentors, poets of immeasurable value, three of whom are on the back of this book (Thomas, Stuart, and David, whose praise I barely deserve), and also: Ruth Stone, Mekeel McBride, Liz Rosenberg, Michael Klein, and Charles Simic. Lastly, my fiancée Mollie, whose support I can only hope to return a small fraction of.

Grateful acknowledgments to the editors of the following publications, where poems in this collection first appeared:

North American Review, winter 2014, "Plenty, Hay"

The Cortland Review, issue 46, "Ain't No Direction But One I Want To Go In, And Can't Never Get There"

2River View, issue 15.2, "Grandpa," and "My Last Words"

Untitled Country Review, "My Father's Garden"

The Lindenwood Review, "Face Down Days"

Pif Magazine, "Float" (reprinted in *Best of Pif 2011*)

CDA News, spring 2012, "Mellowfest"

Spillway, 19, "Blood"

About the Author

Pushcart Prize nominated poet William Stratton spent his formative years on his great-grandfather's farm where he was heavily influenced by the rural landscape and the people native to the area. While his professional career began in journalism, his gradual move towards verse pushed him to pursue an MFA from the University of New Hampshire where he is currently an adjunct professor of writing. William is an advocate of poetry even among those who might not often read it, and believes that poetry belongs to and with all people, not just poets.

www.ingramcontent.com/pod-product-compliance
Lightning Source LLC
Chambersburg PA
CBHW031629040426

42452CB00007B/752